psalms
and
compassions

a jesuit's journey
through cancer

Timothy Brown, S.J.

Library of Congress Card Number: 00-103822
ISBN: 0-9668716-4-2

First Edition, updated
10 9 8 7 6 5 4 3 2 1

Edited by Susan Hodges
Design by resonant design

resonant **publishing**

Baltimore, Maryland
info@resonantgroup.com
www.resonantgroup.com

to my mother...

...and
special thanks to
Susan Hodges,
whose patience and knowledge
helped guide this project
to completion.

table of contents

introduction

—Preface—

This book is borne fruit of a year of recovery after I was given the diagnosis of colon cancer. During this time – before, throughout, and after my surgery – I longed for a book of prayers that focused on healing. After a detailed search, I found what I was looking for in the Book of Psalms.

In reading the Psalms, I came to realize that strength is brought forth by the example and fortification of Christ himself as identified in the Psalms. By enveloping myself in these passages, I was able to become spiritually fortified, enlightened and hopeful in my own recovery.

This book is dedicated to anyone fallen victim to cancer, debilitating diseases, and any form of suffering in which an end seems distant. Stand strong. Breathe hope. Live faith.

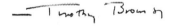

—The Inspiration—

During the course of my illness I turned to the Psalms. I used a wonderful volume, <u>The Psalms with Commentary</u> by Kathleen Norris. In the Introduction to her book, she writes:

The God one encounters in the Psalms is God as human beings have experienced him as both awake and asleep, gloriously present and lamentably absent, and above all, various. A warrior who stands up for us, a mother who holds us to her breast. An eagle sheltering us under her wing, and a creator who brings forth lightning, wind, and rain from the storehouses of heaven. The Psalms work in the way that all great poetry works, allowing us to enter no matter who we are or what we believe, or don't believe; addressing us at the deepest level – what Saint Benedict might term "the ear of the heart." (pp. vii, viii)

I also found myself drawn to the language of the King James version of the Psalms. Why the King James version, with its lack of inclusive language, you might wonder? Again, Kathleen Norris puts it so well:

One reader of a Jesuit magazine wrote an angry letter to complain about an article that had prominently featured a quotation from John Donne: "No man is an island." The editors commented that since Mr. Donne had died in 1631 they had no means of inviting him to revise his grammar for the more "inclusive" modern era. To read and appreciate seventeenth-century verse, or the King James Bible, one must favor imagination over ideology, and discover for oneself the inclusivity that is there. But this is an increasingly difficult task in our literal-minded age. (p. xiv)

But many poets who write in English regard the King James as the literary standard by which to judge subsequent translations of the Bible. The story of this translation – so called because it was commissioned by King James I of England early in the seventeenth century – is a story about the power and primacy of vivid language and pleasurable speech, words that hold the attention of the ear and provide physical images pleasing to the mind's eye. The translation has so embedded itself into the English language that most people are unaware that many images and phrases still in use entered the idiom through the King James: 'my cup runneth over,' 'all flesh is grass,' 'on eagles' wings,' 'tender mercies,' 'loaves and fishes,' 'lilies of the field,' 'salt of the earth,' 'through a glass, darkly,' 'where your treasure is, there will your heart be also.' (p. xvi)

So I ask you to join me in praying through the Psalms – in imagery that is poetic but not inclusive in the literal sense of the meaning. The images evoked are vivid and provide a great deal of comfort. Join me in your prayer.

—Psalm 105—

1.   O give thanks unto the Lord; call upon his name: make known his deeds among the people.

2.   Sing unto him, sing psalms unto him: talk ye of all his wondrous works.

3.   Glory ye in his holy name: let the heart of them rejoice that seek the Lord.

4.   Seek the Lord, and his strength: seek his face evermore.

5.   Remember his marvellous works that he hath done; his wonders, and the judgments of his mouth;

8.   He hath remembered his covenant for ever, the word which he commanded to a thousand generations.

As part of the process for ordination to the priesthood, we, as Jesuits, are asked to write a letter describing what priesthood means to us personally. In my petition letter, I chose the passage taken from the end of John's Gospel where Jesus three times asks Peter: "Do you love me?" And three times tells him: "Feed my lambs... Feed my sheep." Peter responding to Jesus' question passionately answers that he indeed loves the Lord. Thus begins the commission of Peter by Jesus to go out and continue God's work.

Contemplating my priesthood, I realize that the primary task is a gift from God, for which all these years of training could never really even begin to prepare me. That gift is to be sacrament to others. And by sacrament I mean visible sign that God is here – present – in our daily lives – present, too, right here – present as we pray through the Psalms together.

In The Catholic Worker Dorothy Day once wrote about a Jesuit who died many years before I entered the Society. The story goes that this old Jesuit was, in his late years, an incredibly lovable old soul – a perfect follower of Christ. He would go into an old Black hospital in St. Louis – in the days before integration – line up the sick and the insane and baptize them. One old man said about him: "Whenever I open my eyes, there is Father, for he was forever hovering over the people eager to dispense the sacraments to them because that was all he had to give. He couldn't change the rickety old decrepit hospital. He couldn't provide the poor people with decent housing – nor see that they got better jobs. He couldn't seem to do much about making them give up liquor and gambling. No. But he could do one thing – love them – and love them all he did. And he gave them everything he had. He gave them Christ." Some would say he gave them Christ whether they wanted Him or not. But assuredly, these people wanted the old priest's love, and they saw Christ in him when they saw his love for them.

What a lesson that old Jesuit's life is for me and, indeed, for all of us. Giving what we all have the power to give one *another — loving attention and care — something one doesn't need long years of training in philosophy and theology to give. From the time of my diagnosis and all through my recovery the spirit of that holy priest was manifested in the attention given to me by so many.*

diagnosis

—Anima Christi—
St. Ignatius

Soul of Christ, sanctify me.
Body of Christ, save me.
Blood of Christ, inebriate me.
Water from the side of Christ, wash me.
Passion of Christ, strengthen me.
O good Jesus, hear me.
Within your wounds hide me.
Do not allow me to be separated from you.
From the malevolent enemy defend me.
In the hour of my death call me,
and bid me come to you,
that with your saints I may praise you
forever and ever. Amen.

—Psalm 18—

2.   The Lord is my rock, and my fortress, and my deliverer; my God, my strength, in whom I will trust; my buckler, and the horn of my salvation, and my high tower.

3.   I will call upon the Lord, who is worthy to be praised: so shall I be saved from mine enemies.

4.   The sorrows of death compassed me, and the floods of ungodly men made me afraid.

5.   The sorrows of hell compassed me about: the snares of death prevented me.

6.   In my distress I called upon the Lord, and cried unto my God: he heard my voice out of his temple, and my cry came before him, even into his ears.

17.   He delivered me from my strong enemy, and from them which hated me: for they were too strong for me.

18.   They prevented me in the day of my calamity: but the Lord was my stay.

19.   He brought me forth also into a large place; he delivered me, because he delighted in me.

✓ 28.   For thou wilt light my candle: the Lord my God will enlighten my darkness.

29.   For by thee I have run through a troop; and by my God have I leaped over a wall.

In the hardest hours, Lord, when I wasn't sure what the future truly held, I thought the darkest thoughts — dark and depressing thoughts of death, of diminishment, of slowly sinking away. When your strength is sapped, how easy it is to feel this way. I called out in my distress, and was delivered. Delivered from pessimism, delivered from sorrow, from the temptation to give up. With my whole heart I thank you.

—What Cancer Cannot Do—

Cancer is so Limited…
It Cannot Cripple Love,
It Cannot Shatter Hope,
It Cannot Corrode Faith,
It Cannot Destroy Peace,
It Cannot Kill Friendship,
It Cannot Suppress Memories,
It Cannot Invade the Soul,
It Cannot Steal Eternal Life,
It Cannot Conquer the Spirit.

- Anonymous

—Matthew 11:28-30—
The Heart of Christ

Come to me, all you that are weary and are carrying heavy burdens, and I will give you rest. Take my yoke upon you, and learn from me; for I am gentle and humble in heart, and you will find rest for your souls. For my yoke is easy and my burden is light.

hospitalization

—Psalm 6—

2.   Have mercy upon me, O Lord; for I am weak: O Lord, heal me; for my bones are vexed.

3.   My soul is also sore vexed: but thou, O Lord, how long?

4.   Return, O Lord, deliver my soul: oh save me for thy mercies' sake.

5.   For in death there is no remembrance of thee: in the grave who shall give thee thanks?

6.   I am weary with my groaning; all the night make I my bed to swim; I water my couch with my tears.

7.   Mine eye is consumed because of grief; it waxeth old because of all mine enemies.

8.   Depart from me, all ye workers of iniquity, for the Lord hath heard the voice of my weeping.

9.   The Lord hath heard my supplication; the Lord will receive my prayer.

This Psalm speaks for itself. It's okay to feel sorry for yourself – I think. But there is a point where it gets monotonous. I am weary with my own groaning. Take my pain; take my complaining soul. Deliver me from my whining self.

In <u>Waiting for God,</u> Simone Weil develops the theme of attentiveness – the practice of paying attention – in an essay entitled "Reflections on the Right School Studies with a View of the Love of God." She views attention as a kind of waiting, watching and suspended thought. Her point is that we be open – watching and waiting – to receive truth.

Paying attention requires extraordinary concentration and discipline. Weil stresses attention because, for her, prayer consists in just that – attention. She believes that no matter what we are learning and for whatever purpose, the time spent preparing is not wasted because the result will one day be discovered in prayer. But that is not all. She adds that "Not only does the love of God have attention for its substance; the love of our neighbor which we know to be the same love, is made of the same substance. The capacity to give one's attention to a sufferer (to someone in need) is very rare and difficult – almost a miracle and nearly all those who think they have this capacity do not possess it. To give this kind of attention means being able to say to our neighbor: 'What are you going through?'" (<u>Waiting for God</u>, p. 115)

What are you going through? To allow that question to be asked can be a wonderful time of grace for patient and friend alike. Allow the Lord to ask that very question to you. Listen and pray.

—Psalm 88—

1. O Lord God of my salvation, I have cried day and night before thee:

2. Let my prayer come before thee: incline thine ear unto my cry;

3. For my soul is full of troubles: and my life draweth nigh unto the grave.

4. I am counted with them that go down into the pit: I am as a man that hath no strength:

5. Free among the dead, like the slain that lie in the grave, whom thou rememberest no more: and they are cut off from thy hand.

6. Thou hast laid me in the lowest pit, in darkness, in the deeps.

11. Shall thy lovingkindness be declared in the grave? or thy faithfulness in destruction?

12. Shall thy wonders be known in the dark? and thy righteousness in the land of forgetfulness?

13.   But unto thee have I cried, O Lord; and in the morning shall my prayer prevent thee.

14.   Lord, why casteth thou off my soul? why hidest thou thy face from me?

15.   I am afflicted and ready to die from my youth up: while I suffer thy terrors I am distracted.

Sometimes we need a release, a prayer, a great big plea for help. This psalm puts into words those frustrations and desperate thoughts, the agony and despair. It's like a good cry — afterwards you feel so much better.

—Revelations 7:17—

God will wipe away every tear.

—Sirach 2:1-6—

My child, when you come to serve the Lord, prepare yourself for testing.

Set your heart right and steadfast, and do not be impetuous in time of calamity.

Cling to him and do not depart, so that your last days may be prosperous.

Accept whatever befalls you, and in times of humiliation be patient.

For gold is tested in the fire, and those found acceptable, in the furnace of humiliation.

Trust in him, and he will help you; make your ways straight, and hope in him.

The furnace of humiliation!!! Colostomy bags, enemas, poking and prodding, bedpans, hospital gowns, getting assistance in going to the bathroom – humiliations?? This Litany of Humility is certainly fitting for the hospitalized. A great release!

—Private Litany of Humility—

From the desire of being praised, deliver me, Jesus.
From the desire of being honored, deliver me, Jesus.
From the desire of being preferred, deliver me, Jesus.
From the desire of being consulted, deliver me, Jesus.
From the desire of being approved, deliver me, Jesus.
From the desire of comfort and ease, deliver me, Jesus.

From the fear of being humiliated, deliver me, Jesus.
From the fear of being criticized, deliver me, Jesus.
From the fear of being passed over, deliver me, Jesus.
From the fear of being forgotten, deliver me, Jesus.
From the fear of being lonely, deliver me, Jesus.
From the fear of suffering, deliver me, Jesus.

That others may be loved more than I,
    Jesus, grant me the grace to desire it.
That others may be chosen and I set aside,
    Jesus, grant me the grace to desire it.
That others may be praised and I unnoticed,
    Jesus, grant me the grace to desire it.

O Jesus, meek and humble of heart,
    Make my strength like unto Thine.
                Amen.

-Anonymous

—Psalm 117—

1.   O praise the Lord, all ye nations: praise him, all ye people.

2.   For his merciful kindness is great toward us: and the truth of the Lord endureth for ever. Praise ye the Lord.

—Psalm 130—

1.   Out of the depths have I cried unto thee, O Lord.

2.   Lord, hear my voice: let thine ears be attentive to the voice of my supplication.

3.   If thou, Lord, shouldst mark iniquities, O Lord, who shall stand?

4.   But there is forgiveness with thee, that thou mayest be feared.

5.   I wait for the Lord, my soul doth wait, and in his word do I hope.

6.   My soul waiteth for the Lord more than they that watch for the morning: I say, more than they that watch for the morning.

Waiting. Praying. Darkness.
Hope.

—Psalm 13—

1.   How long wilt thou forget me, O Lord? For ever? How long wilt thou hide thy face from me?

2.   How long shall I take counsel in my soul, having sorrow in my heart daily? How long shall mine enemy be exalted over me?

3.   Consider and hear me, O Lord, my God: lighten mine eyes, lest I sleep the sleep of death.

4.   Lest mine enemy say I have prevailed against him; and those that trouble me rejoice when I am moved.

5.   But I have trusted in thy mercy; my heart shall rejoice in thy salvation.

6.   I will sing unto the Lord, because he hath dealt bountifully with me.

I consider the enemy to be the disease. When I do that, it certainly puts the Psalms into a whole different context. When I begin to personalize the sickness as the enemy of all that is whole, healthy, and good, I begin to fight with a focused confidence. God is with me in my struggle to get strong. I ask the Lord to take over and battle for me, and I trust that He will.

—A Prayer in Time of Suffering—

Until my healing comes,
Lord, give me Your grace
so that I may accept my suffering.
Give me your strength so that I
will not despair. Give me your
love so that my suffering may bring me
closer to You, the origin and
source of all love. Amen.

-Anonymous

—Recognizing God in the Most Trivial—
Sacrament of the Present Moment, by Jean Pierre de Caussade, S.J.

To discover God in the smallest and most ordinary things, as well as in the greatest, is to possess a rare and sublime faith. To find contentment in the present moment is to relish and adore the divine will in the succession of all the things to be done and suffered which make up the duty to the present moment. The pure of heart, simple souls, worship God in all the most adverse circumstances; their faith triumphs over everything. The more their senses tell them 'God is not there', the more they drain this cup of bitterness; nothing dismays them, nothing repels them. It was Mary who remained at the foot of the cross when the Apostles fled, and who recognized her son when he was disfigured, spat upon and bruised. It only made him more beloved in the eyes of that tender mother; the more he was blasphemed, the greater her veneration for him. A living faith is nothing else than a steadfast pursuit of God through all that disguises, disfigures, demolishes and seeks, so to speak, to abolish him.

I don't rail out against God. This is not my approach. But here, in this illness, I have the opportunity to again serve God. So Lord, keep my faith strong, so that I continue to see You in the faces of those helping me through this illness — doctors, nurses, friends. Please give me the grace of the present moment to be with You.

—Psalm 3—

3.   But thou, O Lord, art a shield for me; my glory, and the lifter up of mine head.

4.   I cried unto the Lord with my voice, and he heard me out of his holy hill.

5.   I laid me down and slept; I awaked; for the Lord sustained me.

Resting in the Lord – sleeping and waking, sometimes with a morphine drip. But always that sense of God's presence whether asleep or awake. I could sense that God was right there in the room. I lift up my head to look out the hospital window.

—Psalm 42—

1.   As the hart panteth after the water brooks, so pan-
        teth my soul after thee, O God.

2.   My soul thirsteth for God, for the living God:
        when shall I come and appear before God?

3.   My tears have been my meat day and night, while
        they continually say unto me, Where is thy God?

11.   Why art thou cast down, O my soul? And why art
        thou disquieted within me? Hope thou in God:
        for I shall yet praise him, who is the health of my
        countenance, and my God.

*I have so many great memories of deer over the years.
Growing up, crossing on the way to tennis and over to the
swimming pool, we used to pass deer. In tertianship in Los
Gatos, California, the deer would be waiting outside the
chapel during our evening liturgies. One night they filed
up the hill almost in a parallel line as the tertians silently
watched during our thirty day retreat. All nineteen of us
– from all over the world – walked and prayed silently. Even
on retreat at Sag Harbor on Long Island, deer roam the
grounds, almost too friendly (God's delegation).*
        And now in illness I pray Psalm 42. I want to see God,

to see the face of God. I often times think of Teresa of Avila praying for an early death so that she would cut through all the contemplative work to see God face to face. I want to see God, being impatient as I am. But not yet! Heal me.

Yet I do see the face of God — so clearly it is seen in those who surround my bedside in the hospital. I sense God's presence, I see God's face in this compassionate healing.

—Psalm 25—

1.   Unto thee, O Lord, do I lift up my soul.

2.   O my God, I trust in thee: let me not be ashamed, let not mine enemies triumph over me.

4.   Shew me thy ways, O Lord; teach me thy paths.

5.   Lead me in thy truth, and teach me: for thou art the God of my salvation; on thee do I wait all the day.

6.   Remember, O Lord, thy tender mercies and thy lovingkindnesses; for they have been ever of old.

7.   Remember not the sins of my youth, nor my transgressions: according to thy mercy remember thou me for thy goodness' sake, O Lord.

11.   For thy name's sake, O Lord, pardon mine iniquity; for it is great.

15.   Mine eyes are ever toward the Lord; for he shall pluck my feet out of the net.

16.   Turn thee unto me, and have mercy upon me; for I am desolate and afflicted.

17.   The troubles of my heart are enlarged; O bring thou me out of my distresses.

18.   Look upon mine affliction and my pain; and forgive all my sins.

19.   Consider mine enemies; for they are many; and they hate me with cruel hatred.

With a lot of time on my hands, I think back over my life – especially my sins. I begin to pray a life review – examination of conscience. I remember so many good moments with You, Lord, and yet I am sad and ashamed of things that are not of You. I ask forgiveness for my past sins. Pardon me. I am filled with shame and regret.

—The Present Moment Holds Infinite Riches—
Sacrament of the Present Moment, by Jean Pierre de Caussade, S.J.

Nothing is more reasonable, perfect or divine than the will of God. No difference in time, place or circumstance could add to its infinite worth, and if you have been granted the secret of how to discover it in every moment, you have found what is most precious and desirable. God is telling you, that if you abandon all restraint, carry your wishes to their furthest limits, open your heart boundlessly, there is not a single moment when you will not be shown everything you can possibly wish for.

The present moment holds infinite riches beyond your wildest dreams but you will only enjoy them to the extent of your faith and love. The more a soul loves, the more it longs, the more it hopes, the more it finds. The will of God is manifest in each moment, an immense ocean which the heart only fathoms in so far as it overflows with faith, trust and love. The whole of the rest of creation cannot fill your heart, which is larger than all that is not God; terrifying mountains are mere molehills to it. It is in his purpose, hidden in the cloud of all that happens to you in the present moment, that you must rely. You will find it always surpasses your own wishes. Woo no man, worship no shadows or fantasies; they have nothing to offer or accept from you. Only God's purpose can satisfy your longing and leave you nothing to wish for. Adore, walk close to it, see through and abandon all fantasy. Faith is death and destruction to the senses for they worship creatures, whereas faith worships the divine will of God. Discard idols, and the senses will cry like disappointed children, but faith triumphs for it can never be estranged from God's will. When the present moment terrifies, crushes, lays waste and overwhelms the senses, God nourishes, strengthens and revives faith, which, like a general in command of an impregnable position, scorns such useless defenses. (p. 41)

We are always so caught up in what comes next – the next meeting to attend, the next student to counsel, the next issue to address – that we often neglect to pay attention to the moment we are in. One of the graces of illness is that time stretches out before us and we have to slow down. Each moment becomes precious and we can apply all our attention to it. Each moment opens us to God's work in that moment, at that moment – a friend's kind smile, a beautiful flower, a moment of clarity in watching God's will unfold. Rely on God, on the grace in this moment.

recovery

—Psalm 30—

1.   I will extol thee, O Lord; for thou hast lifted me up, and hast not made my foes to rejoice over me.

2.   O Lord my God, I cried unto thee, and thou hast healed me.

3.   O Lord, thou hast brought up my soul from the grave: thou hast kept me alive, that I should not go down to the pit.

4.   Sing unto the Lord, O ye saints of his, and give thanks at the remembrance of his holiness.

10.   Hear, O Lord, and have mercy upon me: Lord, be thou my helper.

11.   Thou hast turned for me my mourning into dancing; thou hast put off my sackcloth, and girded me with gladness;

12.   To the end that my glory may sing praise to thee, and not be silent. O Lord my God, I will give thanks unto thee for ever.

The day I was released from the hospital I praised You,

Lord. But I was very mindful of the nurses, doctors, techni-cians and staff who were so kind and, yes, Christ-like. Each and every one of them. I prayed and named each of them individually before You. I prayed for the treatment, God-like and compassionate, that I received at their hands – the way You worked through them, turning my mourning into dancing.

—Psalm 17—

1. Hear the right, O Lord, attend unto my cry, give ear unto my prayer, that goeth not out of feigned lips.

2. Let my sentence come forth from thy presence; let thine eyes behold the things that are equal.

3. Thou hast proved mine heart; thou hast visited me in the night; thou hast tried me, and shalt find nothing; I am purposed that my mouth shall not transgress.

6. I have called upon thee, for thou wilt hear me, O God: incline thine ear unto me, and hear my speech.

7.   Shew thy marvelous lovingkindness, O thou that savest by thy right hand them which put their trust in thee from those that rise up against them.

8.   Keep me as the apple of the eye, hide me under the shadow of thy wings.

9.   From the wicked that oppress me, from my deadly enemies, who compass me about.

10.   They are inclosed in their own fat: with their mouth they speak proudly.

13.   Arise, O Lord, disappoint him, cast him down: deliver my soul from the wicked, which is thy sword.

This Psalm is filled with so many powerful images. "Thou hast proved mine heart." "Thou hast visited me in the night." "Thou has tried me and shalt find nothing." These verses are particularly comforting. "Thy lovingkindness." "Keep me as the apple of your eye."

Again, how consoling. The images are indescribable; they are images of care, comfort, nourishment and love. Lord, God, you have been there from the start pulling for me, giving me great strength and peace.

Thank you. Gracias.

Amen.

—Sacrament of the Present Moment—
God's Veiled Purpose, by Jean Pierre de Caussade, S.J.

All creatures live by the hand of God. The senses can only grasp the work of man, but faith sees the work of divine action in everything. It sees that Jesus Christ lives in all things, extending his influence over the centuries so that the briefest moment and the tiniest atom contain a portion of that hidden life and its mysterious work. Jesus Christ, after his resurrection, surprised the disciples when he appeared before them in disguise, only to vanish as soon as he had declared himself. The same Jesus still lives and works among us, still surprises souls whose faith is not sufficiently pure and strong. There is no moment when God is not manifest in the form of some affliction, obligation or duty. Everything that happens to us, in us, and through us, embraces and conceals God's divine but veiled purpose, so that we are always being taken by surprise and never recognize it until it has been accomplished. If we could pierce that veil and if we were vigilant and attentive, God would unceasingly reveal himself to us and we would rejoice in his works and in all that happens to us. We would say to everything: 'It is the Lord!' And we would discover that every circumstance is a gift from God; that human beings, frail creatures though they are, will never lack anything; and that God's unceasing concern is to give them what is best for them. If we had faith, we would be grateful to all creatures, we would bless them and inwardly thank them for contributing, under God's hand, so favorably to our perfection. (p. 44)

I am thankful that I am able to offer this pain to Jesus. I have time to think about what purpose this illness might serve — it certainly has slowed me down. I have the opportunity to be grateful for so much, to pay attention to the God who surrounds me. I am reminded of Paul's words to the Corinthians, "...all things are yours...all belong to you, and you belong to Christ, and Christ belongs to God."

restoration

—Psalm 23—

1.   The Lord is my shepherd; I shall not want.

2.   He maketh me to lie down in green pastures: he
       leadeth me beside the still waters.

3.   He restoreth my soul: he leadeth me in the paths of
       righteousness for his name's sake.

4.   Yea, though I walk through the valley of the shadow
       of death, I will fear no evil: for thou art with me;
       thy rod and thy staff they comfort me.

5.   Thou preparest a table before me in the presence
       of mine enemies: thou anointest my head with oil;
       my cup runneth over.

6.   Surely goodness and mercy shall follow me all the
       days of my life: and I will dwell in the house of the
       Lord for ever.

*This Psalm has been a source of consolation for people
in any type of situation. I think of the 23rd Psalm and am
reminded of the Basque shepherd living in Nevada who was
full of legends, mysteries and the religious fervor of his native
Basque homeland.*

I would like to share Fernando D'Alfonso's most remark-able explanation of the 23rd Psalm.

—The Good Shepherd—
Fernando D'Alfonso

The Lord is my Shepherd, I shall not want...

Sheep instinctively know that before they have been folded down for the night that the shepherd has planned out their grazing for the next day. It may be that they are taken back to the same range; it may be that they will go to a new grazing ground. They do not worry. His guidance has been good in the past, and they have faith in the future because they know he has their well-being in view.

He maketh me to lie down in green pastures...

Sheep, grazing from around 3:30 in the morning until about 10:00, are at their most active state. Then they lie down for three or four hours and rest. When they are contentedly chewing their cuds, the shepherd knows they are putting on fat. Consequently the good shepherd starts his flocks out in the earlier hours on the rougher herbage, moving on through the morning to the richer, sweeter grasses, and finally coming to a shady place for the forenoon rest in fine green pastures, the best grazing of the day. Sheep resting in such happy surroundings feel contentment.

He leadeth me beside the still waters...

Every shepherd knows that sheep will not drink gurgling water. There are many small springs high in the hills of the Holy Land, whose waters run down the valleys only to evaporate in the desert sun. Although the sheep need the water, they will not drink from these fast-flowing springs and streams. The shepherd must find a place where rocks or erosion have made a little pool, or else he fashions with his hands a pocket sufficient to hold at least a bucketful.

He restoreth my soul. He leadeth me in the paths of righteousness for his name's sake...

In the Holy Land each sheep takes his place in the grazing line in the morning and keeps the same position throughout the day. Once during the day, however, each sheep leaves its place and goes to the shepherd. Whereupon the shepherd stretches out his hand and rubs the animal's nose and ears, scratches its chin, whispers affectionately into its ears. The sheep, meanwhile, rubs its cheeks against his face. After a few minutes of this communion with the Master, the sheep returns to its place in the feeding line.

Yea, though I walk through the valley of the shadow of death, I will fear no evil: for thou art with me; thy rod and thy staff they comfort me...

There is an actual Valley of the Shadow of Death in Palestine, and every shepherd from Spain to Dalmatia knows of it. It is south of Jericho Road leading from Jerusalem to the Dead Sea, and it is narrow — a narrow defile — through a mountain range. Climatic and grazing conditions make it necessary for the sheep to be moved through this valley for seasonal feeding each year. The valley is four and one half miles long. Its side walls are over 1,500 feet high in places, and it is only 10 or 12 feet wide at the bottom. Travel through the valley is dangerous because its floor has gullies seven or eight feet deep. Actual footing on solid rock is so narrow in many places that a sheep cannot turn around, and it is an unwritten law of the shepherds that flocks must go up the valley in the morning hours and down toward eventide, lest flocks meet in the defile.

About half way through the valley the walk crosses from one side to the other at a place where the path is cut in two by an eight foot gully. One side of the gully is about 18 inches higher than the other; the sheep must jump across it. The shepherd stands at this break and coaxes or forces the sheep to make the leap. If a sheep slips and lands in the gully the shepherd's rod is brought into play. The old style crook circles a large sheep's neck or a small sheep's chest, and the animal is lifted to safety. If a more modern crook is used, the sheep is caught about the hoofs and lifted up to safety. Many wild dogs lurk in the shadows of the valley, looking for prey. The shepherd, skilled in throwing his staff, uses it as a weapon. Thus the sheep have learned to fear no evil in the Valley of the Shadow of Death, for their Master is there to protect them from harm.

Thou preparest a table before me in
the presence of mine enemies:..

David's meaning is a simple one when conditions in the Holy Land sheep ranges are known. Poisonous plants which are fatal to grazing animals abound. Each spring the shepherd must be constantly alert. When he finds the plants, he takes his mattock and goes on ahead of the flock, grubbing out every stock and root he can see. As he digs out the stocks he lays them upon little stones, some of which were built by shepherds in Old Testament days, and by the morrow they are dry enough to burn. When the pasture is free of poisonous plants, the sheep are led into it, and in the presence of their "plant-enemies," they eat in peace.

Thou anointest my head with oil;
my cup runneth over...

At every sheepfold there is a big earthen bowl of olive oil and a large jar of water. As the sheep come in for the night, they are led to the gate. The shepherd lays his rod across the top of the gateway just above the backs of the sheep. As each sheep passes he quickly examines it for briars in the ears, snags in the cheek or weeping of the eyes from dust or scratches. When such conditions are found, he drops the rod across the sheep's back and it steps out of line. Each sheep's wounds are carefully cleaned. Then the shepherd dips his hand into the olive oil and anoints the injury. A large cup is dipped into the jar of water kept cool by evaporation in the unglazed pottery, and is brought over – never half-full, but always overflowing. The sheep will sink its nose into the water, clear to the eyes if fevered, and drink until refreshed. When all the sheep are at rest, the shepherd places his staff within reach in case it is needed during the night. Then he wraps himself in his woolen robe and lies down across the gateway, facing the sheep for his night's repose.

So after all the care and protection shown by the shepherd, I may join in the Psalm of David and say:

Surely goodness and mercy shall follow me
all the days of my life:
and I will dwell in the house of the Lord for ever.

—The Communion of Saints—

My friend Thérèse was diagnosed with ALS (Lou Gehrig's disease), and as I visited her many times as she progressed through the stages of this disease, I watched her suffer. But I was in awe of the way she incorporated her faith into her illness. Throughout her sickness she drew on her friends' prayers as a living Communion of Saints. And now her friendship takes on a new dimension. All of our friends who have suffered and died become part of our Communion of Saints to whom we can then turn. This personal connection to the Communion of Saints was a real source of courage to me. This letter from Thérèse was written shortly before her death. She, too, prayed the Psalms during the long course of her illness.

Letter from Thérèse, December 1994
Dear Friends and Family,

This Advent, season of waiting, has been a very special one for me. A long time ago I used to like a phrase from The Grail: "All of life is an Advent...We are always waiting for Christ to come to us."

With the progression of the ALS, I am well aware that I am waiting for Him to come to bring me home. I don't say this in a morbid way but full of hope and trust. Pray with me that as the disease takes my voice and swallowing that the grace of hope and trust will be given me especially.

My favorite words this Advent arose from my heart because of my lived experience and I'd like to share them with you.

#1 – "Prepare the way of the Lord...Make the rough ways smooth." My growing up Irish in the '40s left me with certain prejudices: misunderstanding of Orientals and great inhibitions about those who have physical or mental disability. These are some of my "rough places" (Since this isn't confession, I'm not listing all of them!). However, this past year I've been gifted with a generous, fun-loving straightforward Korean woman and this experience shattered my misconceptions about Orientals. In my work at Villanova I was always reluctant to give myself wholeheartedly to the part of my job where I was to work with those who had physical disabilities less I not know what to do for them. As I have become progressively more disabled, I am learning that those with disabilities are primarily people like all others who only happen to have disabilities. In November I was invited "to tell my story" at The Handicapped Encounter Christ retreat. I went hesitantly knowing I needed to be there for my own inner healing. The warm, loving heartfelt acceptance given me by those with physical disabilities brought tears to my eyes and melted my heart. Within two minutes I felt "at home" and in the midst of family though I only knew one person in the group of those with disabilities, yet another rough edge smoothed out!

#2 – "The Word was made flesh and pitched His tent in our midst." For me He has taken flesh concretely in the many visits and experiences I've had since I came to the nursing home. The daily flow of faithful friends (from Warminster, The Assumption, Wernersville, Villanova, and Lansdale) keep on reminding me of the boundless limits of His love manifested in their kindness, compassion, and fidelity.

My weekly visits for aqua therapy and my massages enable me to focus on my body become FLESH, and remind me of the Treasure that I carry in a very broken and weak vessel. The generosity of so many people who have made the therapy and massage possible touches me beyond words – another way for me to learn to RECEIVE humbly and gratefully.

#3 – "Mary kept all these things pondering them in her heart." I have only touched on some of the heart-warming experiences with which I have been spoiled. I have many hours in which to ponder now that my arms and legs leave me inactive and my voice is weakening. Being who I am, I cry and have tantrums several times a day. Fortunately, they only last a few minutes because Thérèse, the real one, helps me remember the many positive, consoling proofs of love which far outweigh my progressive debilitation. In my better moments and there are many, I ponder the richness of my many, many loved ones – those who write, those who visit or call, and the old faithfuls who take care of all my needs physical and other.

All of this — an exceedingly long missive — is to tell you how my Advent has gone, and so I only have left my loving wishes and prayers for a peace-filled, joy-full Christmas! May He continue to come to all of us in our daily experience and give us the grace to recognize Him!

All of life is an Advent. We are always waiting for Christ to come to us. Prepare the way of the Lord. Make the rough ways smooth. How I prayed with Thérèse and asked for her support as someone who was taught by God to wait in patient hope. Thérèse's great devotion to St. Thérèse the Little Flower kept her focused through to the end. Every month a rose arrived at the nursing home (I was in on the secret, she never knew where the rose came from).

That preparation — preparation and waiting were a great source of consolation and peace for me. Watching and waiting — the preparation of letting go — telling God to take over.

—Psalm 97—

10.   Ye that love the Lord, hate evil: he preserveth the souls of his saints; he delivereth them out of the hand of the wicked.

11.   Light is sown for the righteous, and gladness for the upright in heart.

12.   Rejoice in the Lord, ye righteous; and give thanks at the remembrance of his holiness.

I pray for the grace to age well, to be a good patient. In diminishment I pray for the grace of a strong faith. There are people who surround me, who exhibit a deep faith, and it is amazingly contagious. It is catching; it is uplifting and calming.

A true Communion of Saints surrounds me. Then there are the great saints who strengthen me with their powerful prayers and intercessions. Here are a few: three saints in this communion – St. Augustine, St. Thérèse the Little Flower, and St. Teresa of Avila. Hear their consoling words.

—St. Augustine—

My heart lies before you, O my God.
        Look deep within –
        See these memories of mine,
        for you are my hope.
You cleanse me when unclean humors
such as these possess me.
By drawing my eyes to yourself
and saving my feet from the snare.

—Therese of Lisieux—

My life is an instant – a fleeting now.
My life is a moment, which swiftly escapes me.
O my God, you know that
on earth I have only today to love you. Amen.

—Teresa's Bookmark—

Let nothing trouble you
Let nothing scare you
All is fleeting
God alone is unchanging
Patience
Everything obtains
Who possesses God
Nothing wants
God alone suffices.

—Teresa of Avila—

I am yours and born for you
What do you want of me?
Yours – you made me
Yours – you saved me
Yours – you endured me
Yours – you called me
Yours – you awaited
Yours – I did not stray
What do you want of me?

—Psalm 103—
Psalm of David

1. Bless the Lord, O my soul: and all that is within me, bless his holy name.

2. Bless the Lord, O my soul, and forget not all his benefits:

3. Who forgiveth all thine iniquities; who healeth all thy diseases;

4. Who redeemeth thy life from destruction; who crowneth thee with lovingkindness and tender mercies;

5. Who satisfieth thy mouth with good things; so that thy youth is renewed like the eagle's.

8. The Lord is merciful and gracious, slow to anger, and plenteous in mercy.

11. For as the heaven is high above the earth, so great is his mercy toward them that fear him.

To bless – in Latin, bene dicere *– to say good things. Bless – praise – forget not all His benefits. The benefits: forgiveness, redemption, tender mercy. When you have a lot of time on your hands it is amazing what memories come to mind. Praying back and remembering forward; hoping back and loving forward. A wonderful dynamic of grace.*

Lord, forget not the benefits, give me strength, the ability to hope, blessings of a life of all the good gifts you bestowed. I think of Rabbi Heschel and the stirring words he spoke when recovering from heart surgery: "Just to be is a blessing." To be – remembering forward, hoping backward – a great grace.

—Principle and Foundation—
From The Spiritual Exercises of St. Ignatius

Human beings are created to praise, reverence, and serve God our Lord, and by means of doing this to save their souls.

The other things on the face of the earth are created for the human beings, to help them in the pursuit of the end for which they are created.

From this it follows that we ought to use these things to the extent that they help us toward our end, and free ourselves from them to the extent that they hinder us from it.

To attain this it is necessary to make ourselves indifferent to all created things, in regard to everything which is left to our free will and is not forbidden. Consequently, on our own part we ought not to seek health rather than sickness, wealth rather than poverty, honor rather than dishonor, a long life rather than a short one, and so on in all other matters.

Rather, we ought to desire and choose only that which is more conducive to the end for which we are created.

A few years ago, Joe Grady, Jesuit scholastic, age 32, was buried at Wernersville. In December 1985, during his second year of regency at St. Joe's Prep, he was told he had leukemia. The disease progressed and during his first year of theology, he made the decision to undergo a bone marrow transplant.

Later that year he would receive new marrow from his younger sister, Colleen. The transplant was successful, but some months afterwards, Joe contracted viral pneumonia from which he never recovered.

At the cemetery, Joe's mother read a passage written by another Maryland Province Jesuit, buried only a few feet away from Joe. It was a passage she had read to Joe in the hospital at the point when Joe was no longer able to read – although still very much alert and aware. The other Jesuit was Walter Ciszek. The book – <u>He Leadeth Me</u> – was Father Ciszek's account of his 23 years in the Soviet Union most of which was spent in prison or slave labor camps in Siberia.

Two Jesuits – two different generations – two very different experiences and worlds – both shared something. Both lived under the same Principle and Foundation ... That Principle – that we are created to praise, reverence, and serve God our Lord, and by this means to save our souls. The other things on the face of the earth are created for us to help us in attaining the end for which we are created. And so, we are to make use of them insofar as they help us in the attainment of our end, and we must rid ourselves of them insofar as they prove a hindrance to us.

Therefore we must make ourselves indifferent to all created things as far as we are allowed free choice and are not under any prohibition. Consequently as far as we are concerned we should not prefer health to sickness, riches to poverty, honor to dishonor, a long life to a short life. The same holds for all other things. Our one desire and choice should be what is more conducive to the end for which we are created.

The Principle and Foundation – a real challenge – Joe Grady knew that. He lived that with real heart, great humor, deep faith. And he struggled as I think all of us do. For are we really meant to believe we should prefer a short life to a long life? Poverty to riches? Sickness to health? Are we able to embrace the Cross? Even celebrate the Cross? Place ourselves with Christ crucified in this world today?

Walter Ciszek appreciated those words as well. He knew the meaning of the Principle and Foundation and certainly lived them out for so many years imprisoned, having little to eat, working long hours, being forced to say Mass secretly with a few others – secretly taking the crusts of bread at breakfast and saving them until he got back at night. Polish prisoners would make wine out of stolen raisins – a cover for a gold watch would serve as a paten. The chalice a shotglass. Back home in the Maryland Province he would be officially listed as dead and added to the list of Masses Jesuits said for the repose of souls. In those dark days for Fr. Ciszek, when the temptation to give up was so present, he was able to call to mind the end for which he was made – he looked to God's Providence.

In the last few months of his life, Joe Grady would hear those words of Ciszek's read to him by his mother. She shared one of those passages with all of us that July. From the Epilogue of <u>He Leadeth Me</u>, Father Ciszek wrote: What I have tried to show in the pages of this book, however, is how faith has affected my life and sustained me in all I experienced. That faith is the answer to the question most often asked of me – 'How did you manage to survive?' And I can only repeat it, simply and unashamedly. To me the truth says more than that man has a duty and obligation toward his Creator, as *many have tended to interpret it. To me, it says that God has a special purpose, a special love, a special providence for all those He has created...It means for example that every moment of our life has a purpose. That every action of ours, no matter how dull or routine or trivial it may seem in itself, has a dignity and a worth beyond human understanding. Yet what a terrible responsibility is here. For it means that no moment can be wasted, no opportunity missed.*

That was the secret Walter Ciszek came to know. He would say that it was not his alone — Christ spoke of it, the saints have practiced it, and I think Joe Grady came to know that secret in his own courageous suffering.

—Late have I loved you—
St. Augustine

Late have I loved you, O beauty ever ancient, ever new!
Late have I loved you.
And behold, you were within, and I without,
   and without I sought you.
And deformed, I ran after those forms of beauty
   you have made.
You were with me, and I was not with you,
   those things held me back from you,
   things whose only being was to be in you.
You called; you cried;
   and you broke through my deafness.
You flashed; you shone;
   and you chased away my blindness.
You became fragrant;
   and I inhaled and sighed for you.
I tasted, and now hunger and thirst for you.
You touched me; and I burned for your embrace.

—A Prayer for Healing—

O mother of mercy,
   health of the sick,
   refuge of sinners,
   comforter of the afflicted,
   You know my wants,
   my troubles, my sufferings,
Look with mercy on me.
By appearing at the Grotto of Lourdes -
   you were pleased to make a privileged sanctuary,
   where you disperse your favors.
I pray with complete confidence to
   implore your intercession.

                            -Anonymous

—Way of Light - Via Lucis—

The traditional Via Crucis (Way of the Cross) ends with Christ's burial. The Salesian order in Rome, picking up from the end of the traditional Stations of the Cross, has inaugurated 14 new stations focusing on Christ's Resurrection and Ascension and his sending the Holy Spirit.

The Salesians chose the catacombs as the site for the new stations as a reminder that the remains rest there in expectation of their resurrection at the end of time.

The Stations of the Cross are popular because people today are suffering greatly and can identify with Jesus' passion. But Jesus told his disciples, "I am the Resurrection and the life." Christians are called not only to pick up their own crosses and follow Jesus, but to be witnesses to the fact that suffering and death are not the end of the journey.

The Way of Light – what a hope-filled image. It is really important to remember that our lives do not end in suffering and death, but rather in the hope of Resurrection. God leads us through our human suffering, to everlasting union with Him. It is through His gift to us of His most precious Son that we can experience that union.

The 14 stations of the Via Lucis are:

1)   Jesus rises from the dead
2)   The disciples discover the empty tomb
3)   The risen Jesus appears to Mary Magdalen
4)   Jesus walks with the disciples on the road to Emmaus
5)   Jesus reveals himself in the breaking of the bread
6)   Jesus shows the disciples he is alive
7)   Jesus gives his disciples the power to forgive sins
8)   The risen Lord confirms the faith of Thomas
9)   Jesus meets the disciples by the Sea of Tiberius
10)   Jesus confirms the primacy of Peter
11)   Jesus tells the apostles to make disciples of all nations
12)   Jesus ascends into heaven
13)   With Mary, the disciples await the Holy Spirit
14)   Jesus sends his Holy Spirit to the disciples

—Prayer to the Holy Spirit—

O Holy Spirit, give me stillness of soul in you.
Calm the turmoil within with the gentleness of
  your peace.
Quiet the anxiety within with a deep trust in you.
Heal the wounds of sin within with the joy of your
  forgiveness.
Strengthen the faith within with the awareness of
  your presence.
Confirm the hope within with the knowledge of
  your strength.
Give fullness to the love within with an outpouring
  of your love.
O Holy Spirit, be to me a source of light, strength
  and courage so that I may hear your call ever
  more clearly and follow it more generously. Amen.

-Anonymous

—Healing—

O Little Flower of Jesus, ask God today to grant the healing I seek. I now place my urgent request with confidence in your hands so that I may be renewed in body, mind and spirit and receive the healing I so desperately desire.

-Anonymous

chemotherapy

—Psalm 31—

9.   Have mercy upon me, O Lord, for I am in trouble:
       mine eye is consumed with grief, yea, my soul and
       my belly.

10.   For my life is spent with grief, and my years with
       sighing: my strength faileth because of mine iniq-
       uity, and my bones are consumed.

*In times of pain, in times of distress, I would pray Psalm
31. I think especially of the times of chemotherapy; feeling
the nausea and exhaustion and having only a little strength,
I would ask for strength and pity. Pity and strength are the
words that stand out here. My strength is sapped, but with
God there, I feel okay. My strength yields, but not to misery.
My strength yields to God.*

—Psalm 61—

1.   Hear my cry, O God; attend unto my prayer.

2.   From the end of the earth will I cry unto thee,
       when my heart is overwhelmed: lead me to the rock
       that is higher than I.

3.   For thou hast been a shelter for me, and a strong
       tower from the enemy.

4.   I will abide in thy tabernacle for ever: I will trust in
       the covert of thy wings.

5.   For thou, O God, hast heard my vows: thou hast
       given me the heritage of those that fear thy name.

6.   Thou wilt prolong the king's life: and his years as
       many generations.

7.   He shall abide before God for ever: O prepare
       mercy and truth, which may preserve him.

8.   So will I sing praise unto thy name for ever, that I
       may daily perform my vows.

*During the hours of chemotherapy when the I.V. is
hooked up and the chemicals are streaming through my
veins, I would pray to Mary. Often I would be surrounded
by people who looked much sicker than I felt. Often I would
pray the Rosary, asking the Blessed Mother to be with all
of us in the room, all of us hooked up, especially those who
were close to death.*

Hail Mary,
Full of grace,
The Lord is with thee.
Blessed art thou among women,
And blessed is the fruit of thy womb,
Jesus.

Holy Mary, Mother of God,
Pray for us sinners,
Now and at the hour of our death. Amen.

—Prayer for the Sick—

Dear Jesus –

   Healer of the sick,
I turn to you in this time of
illness. Alleviate my worry and
sorrow with Your gentle love and
grant me the grace and strength
to accept this Burden.
   I place my worries in Your hands.
I place myself in Your love and humbly
ask that You restore Your servant to
health again.
   Above all, grant me the
grace to acknowledge Your holy will
and know that You love me and are
with me in this, my most difficult time.
   Amen.

                              -Anonymous

—Psalm 116—

1.   I love the Lord, because he hath heard my voice and my supplications.

2.   Because he hath inclined his ear unto me, therefore will I call upon him as long as I live.

3.   The sorrows of death compassed me, and the pains of hell gat hold upon me: I found trouble and sorrow.

4.   Then called I upon the name of the Lord; O Lord, I beseech thee, deliver my soul.

5.   Gracious is the Lord, and righteous; yea, our God is merciful.

6.   The Lord preserveth the simple: I was brought low, and he helped me.

7.   Return unto thy rest, O my soul; for the Lord hath dealt bountifully with thee.

8.   For thou hast delivered my soul from death, mine eyes from tears, and my feet from falling.

9.   I will walk before the Lord in the land of the living.

10.   I believed, therefore have I spoken: I was greatly afflicted:

13.   I will take the cup of salvation, and call upon the name of the Lord.

14.   I will pay my vows unto the Lord now in the presence of all his people.

15.   Precious in the sight of the Lord is the death of his saints.

16.   O Lord, truly I am thy servant; I am thy servant, and the son of thine handmaid: thou hast loosed my bonds.

17.   I will offer to thee the sacrifice of thanksgiving, and will call upon the name of the Lord.

18.   I will pay my vows unto the Lord now in the presence of all his people.

Praying through Psalm 116 I saw a real connection with patient trust with the emphasis on <u>patient</u>. Anyone who knows me can tell you that patience is not my greatest virtue. Patience for this <u>patient</u> is something for which I would pray. Psalm 116 speaks to that desire to be low key and easy in my desire to trust in God's healing power. I beseech thee, deliver my soul. I believe for thou hast delivered my soul from death.

One of my favorite prayers has always been Teilhard de Chardin's "Patient Trust in Ourselves and the Slow Work of God." Over the years I have photocopied this prayer and sent it to people dealing with all kinds of hard personal situations.

—Patient Trust—
Pierre Teilhard de Chardin, S.J.

Above all, trust in the slow work of God,
We are, quite naturally,
impatient in everything to reach the end
without delay.

We should like to skip the intermediate stages
We are impatient of being
on the way to something unknown,
something new,
And yet it is the law of all progress
that is made by passing through
some stages of instability —
And that it may take a very long time.

And so I think it is with you.
Your ideas mature gradually,
let them grow,
let them shape themselves,
without undue haste.

Don't try to force them on,
as though you could be today
what time (that is to say, grace and
circumstances acting
on your own good will)
will make you tomorrow.

Only God could say what this new spirit
gradually forming within you will be
Give our Lord the benefit of believing
that his band is leading you,
and accept the anxiety of
feeling yourself in suspense and incomplete.

—Most Sacred Heart of Jesus—

I come to you in my need
Keep me close to you and accept the pain and suffering I
offer you today.
I unite it with your own offering to the Father.

Heart of Jesus, watch over my loved ones.
Feed your poor and hungry people.
Give me strength and see me to health if it is your will.
Above all grant me always the grace to trust in your promise
of love.

Most Loving Heart of Jesus
Bring me health in body and spirit that I may serve you
with all my strength. Touch gently this life which you have
created.

-Anonymous

*Testing and trials. So many people come to say, why did
God do this? I have never really thought of it that way. I
never really saw God as causing my illness, or that my cancer
is somehow a test. I never have struggled much with that.
Other things, yes; but not that.*

—Psalm 144—

1.   Blessed be the Lord my strength, which teacheth my hands to war, and my fingers to fight:

2.   My goodness, and my fortress; my high tower, and my deliverer; my shield, and he in whom I trust; who subdueth my people under me.

3.   Lord, what is man, that thou takest knowledge of him! or the son of man, that thou makest account of him!

4.   Man is like to vanity: his days are as a shadow that passeth away.

5.   Bow thy heavens, O Lord, and come down: touch the mountains, and they shall smoke.

6.   Cast forth lightning, and scatter them: shoot out thine arrows, and destroy them.

7.   Send thine hand from above; rid me, and deliver me out of great waters, from the hand of strange children.

8.   Whose mouth speaketh vanity, and their right hand is a right hand of falsehood.

9.   I will sing a new song unto thee, O God: upon a psaltery and an instrument of ten strings will I sing praises unto thee.

10.   It is he that giveth salvation unto kings: who delivereth David his servant from the hurtful sword.

11.   Rid me, and deliver me from the hand of strange children, whose mouth speaketh vanity, and their right hand is a right hand of falsehood:

12.   That our sons may be as plants grown up in their youth; that our daughters may be as corner stones, polished after the similitude of a palace:

13.   That our garners may be full, affording all manner of store: that our sheep may bring forth thousands and ten thousands in our streets:

14.   That our oxen may be strong to labour; that there be no breaking in, nor going out; that there be no complaining in our streets.

15.   Happy is that people, that is in such a case: yea, happy is that people, whose God is the Lord.

I pray for those enduring a much harsher treatment than I am experiencing. I pray for you mothers, middle-aged fathers, grandmothers, aunts and uncles, friends — all sitting and I.V.'d and in pain. Exhausted, hope-fallen. I see your hope, the child's love in accompanying you. I pray that your sons may be as plants growing up with you, and your daughters as corner stones, polished like a palace. I pray that all of you here may be restored to full health so that you can see your children's children thrive and grow and love.

Happy indeed is that people whose God is the Lord.
Teach our hands to war and our fingers to fight
     ...the disease
     ...the anxiety
     ...the fear
     ...the desire to be productive and active again
     ...the pain
     ...the frustration...

In chemotherapy I pray that you cast forth lightning in that poisonous drip — scatter and kill the deadly disease. Shoot out arrows — destroy the enemy — the cancer cell.

—Heart of Jesus—

The heart of Jesus
is overflowing with
compassion for all those who suffer
those beset by troubles, difficulties
and hardships.

His is the heart of a father
the heart of a mother
the heart of a shepherd.

-Anonymous

—A Lesson—

In John's Gospel the Spirit is called the Paraclete. There is no exact English translation for the Greek Paraclete. Sometimes it is translated as advocate – someone who speaks for another; sometimes it is translated as defender – someone who acts on one's behalf, one's counselor. But perhaps the closest we can get to the meaning of the word is the one who spurs runners on in a race. The Paraclete is like an athlete's trainer. The Paraclete stands at the side of the track and encourages the runners. You can do it, go for it, go for the gold. Paraclete is the spur, that driving vision; the Spirit is the one who pushes us. The image takes off!

ponderings

I think of Pierre Teilhard de Chardin's Prayer of Diminishment. I first remember hearing this prayer around the time Father Joe Sellinger, S.J., the President of Loyola College from 1964-1993, was dying of pancreatic cancer. It was incorporated into a homily given by the College Rector at a memorial Mass. I still find it stirring to this very day. The grace of diminishment – something for which to pray.

Teilhard de Chardin offers some extraordinary thoughts on the process of spiritual healing:

—Prayer of Diminishment—
Pierre Teilhard de Chardin, S.J.

When the signs of age begin to mark my body
(and still more when they touch my mind);
when the ill that is to diminish me or carry me off
strikes from without or is born within me;
when the painful moment comes
in which I suddenly awaken
to the fact that I am ill or growing old;
and above all at that last moment
when I feel I am losing hold of myself
and am absolutely passive within the hands
of the great unknown forces that have formed me;
in all those dark moments, O God,
grant that I may understand that it is You
(provided only my faith is strong enough)
who are painfully parting the fibres of my being
in order to penetrate to the very marrow
of my substance and bear me away within yourself.

—The Significance and Positive Value of Suffering—
Pierre Teilhard de Chardin, S.J.

All the sufferers of the earth joining their sufferings so that the world's pain might become a great and unique act of consciousness, elevation and union. Would not this be one of the highest forms that the mysterious work of creation could take in our sight?

—The Heart of Matter—
Pierre Teilhard de Chardin, S.J.

When all is said and done, I can see this: I managed to climb up to the point where the Universe became apparent to me as a great rising surge, in which all the work that goes into serious inquiry, all the will to create, all the acceptance of suffering, converge ahead into a single dazzling spear-head — now, at the end of my life, I can stand on the peak I have scaled and continue to look ever more closely into the future, and there, with ever more assurance, see the assent of God.

—In the Shadow—
Pierre Teilhard de Chardin, S.J.

In the shadow of death may we not look back to the past, but seek in utter darkness the dawn of God.

—Colossians 1:24—

I am now rejoicing in my sufferings for your sake, and in my flesh I am completing what is lacking in Christ's afflictions for the sake of His body, that is, the church.

I think of Teresa of Avila and all that she wrote about suffering and the contemplative life in Christ. After all those years of reading and praying about suffering with the crucified Christ, I now catch a slight glimpse. Just an idea of His immense redemptive love slowly seeps into my consciousness and on down deeper into my soul.

—Words of Advice from Teresa of Avila—

The story is told that when Saint Teresa of Avila was a child, she and her brother, Rodrigo, went off toward the country of the Moors in the hope that there they would have their heads cut off. The two fugitives were overtaken by an uncle who brought them back home. To the anxious parents, asking why they ran away, Teresa answered, "I went because I want to see God, and to see God, we must die."

And so early on in her life, she set out to seek God — to see God. Later on she would enter Carmel where she continued her quest.

It took her many years to get to the point where she could experience the living God in her life ... but finally she got to the point where she felt the presence of Jesus 'like a person in a dark room whom you cannot see but you know is there.'

And isn't that what we are all about — seeking God — seeking the face of God in all that we do and with everyone we come to meet? The question is how do we see God.

The following are some wonderful lines, ponderings for the healing heart taken from the writings of Teresa of Avila:

—Contemplative Words of Teresa of Avila—

We shouldn't build castles in the air. The Lord doesn't look so much at the greatness of our works as at the love with which they are done. *(The Interior Castle)*

Some books on prayer tell us where one must seek God. Within oneself, very clearly, is the best place to look. *(The Book of Her Life)*

Many remain at the foot of the mount who could ascend to the top...I repeat and ask that you always have courageous thoughts. As a result of them the Lord will give you grace for courageous deeds. *(Meditations on the Song of Songs)*

What would it matter, when you are in the arms of God if the whole world blame you! *(The Way of Perfection)*

O How everything that is suffered with love is healed again. *(The Way of Perfection)*

And even in sickness itself and these other occasions the prayer is genuine when it comes from a soul that loves to offer the sickness up and accept what is happening and be conformed to it and to the other thousand things that happen. *(The Book of Her Life)*

LOVE TURNS WORK INTO REST. *(Soliloquies)*

In the measure you desire Him, you will find Him. *(The Way of Perfection)*

Not with the noise of words, but with longing that He hears us. *(The Book of Her Life)*

What folly: to flee from the Light so as to be always stumbling! *(The Book of Her Life)*

If you do not strive for the virtues and practice them, you will always be dwarfs. *(The Interior Castle)*

In order to ascend to the dwelling places we desire, the important thing is not to think much but to love much: and so do what best stirs you to love. *(The Interior Castle)*

Now, is Your Face such, Lord, that we would not look at it when You are so close to us? And do we close our eyes to avoid seeing that You, Lord, are looking at us? *(The Way of Perfection)*

He never tires of giving…let us not tire of receiving. *(The Book of Her Life)*

In the measure you desire Him, you will find Him. *(The Way of Perfection)*

For mental prayer in my opinion is nothing else than an intimate sharing between friends, it means taking time frequently to be alone with Him who we know. *(The Book of Her Life)*

He will see that whoever loves Him much will be able to suffer much for Him, whoever loves Him little will be capable of little. I myself hold that the measure for being able to bear a large or small cross is love. *(The Way of Perfection)*

A good means to having God is to speak with His friends. *(The Way of Perfection)*

Prayer and comfortable living are incompatible. *(The Way of Perfection)*

Yes, bring yourselves to consider and understand whom you are speaking with, or, as you approach, with whom you are about to speak. *(The Way of Perfection)*

Life is but a night spent in an uncomfortable inn, crowded together with other wayfarers. *(The Way of Perfection)*

This body has one fault, that the more people pamper it, the more its wants are known. It is strange how much it likes to be indulged. How well it finds some good pretext to deceive the poor soul. *(The Interior Castle)*

—The Communion of Saints—

We pray for the departed because we love them in the love that comes from God. And believing them to be nearer God than we are, we are sure that they pray for us more strongly within that same love. To ask the departed to pray for us and ourselves to pray for them is a natural expression of our solidarity with them in the redemptive love of God in Christ. Because of the sense of union linking all Christians, both living and dead, the Church has from the first ages cultivated with great piety the memory of the dead through the offering of prayers on their behalf. When we look at the lives of those who have faithfully followed Christ, we are inspired. God vividly speaks to us in those who shared our humanity and yet are transformed into successful images of Christ.

—Psalm 100—

1.   Make a joyful noise unto the Lord, all ye lands.

2.   Serve the Lord with gladness: come before his presence with singing.

3.   Know ye that the Lord he is God: it is he that hath made us, and not we ourselves; we are his people, and the sheep of his pasture.

4.   Enter into his gates with thanksgiving, and into his courts with praise: be thankful unto him, and bless his name.

5.   For the Lord is good; his mercy is everlasting; and his truth endureth to all generations.

—A Prayer for Healing—

Lord -
You invite all who are burdened to come to You.
Allow Your healing hand to heal me.
Touch my soul with Your compassion for others -
Touch my heart with Your courage and infinite love
for all.

Touch my mind with Your wisdom,
that my mouth may always proclaim Your praise.

Teach me to reach out to You in my need,
and help me to lead others to You by my example.

Most loving Heart of Jesus,
bring me health in body and spirit
that I may love You with all my strength.

Touch gently this life which You have created,
Now and forever - Amen.

-Anonymous

—Sirach 7 : 5- 9, 14-17—
True Friendship

A kind mouth multiplies friends,
>   and gracious lips prompt friendly
>   greetings.
Let your acquaintances be many,
>   but one in a thousand your confidant.
When you gain a friend, first test him,
>   and be not too ready to trust him.
For one sort of friend is a friend when it
>   suits him,
>   but he will not be with you in time of
>   distress.
A faithful friend is a sturdy shelter;
>   he who finds one finds a treasure.
A faithful friend is beyond price,
>   no sum can balance his worth.
A faithful friend is a life-saving remedy,
>   such as he who fears God finds;
For he who fears God behaves accordingly,
>   and his friend will be like himself.

This is a passage that I often recommend to couples as their first Reading for their wedding Mass. It is a favorite reading for many couples because they view their married love based in friendship – love connected to friendship.

Friends in Christ; God's friends. I reflect on all the

people who are with me through this illness. God's love and divinity is so brightly mirrored in the kindness of friends. Friends' thoughtfulness – bringing food and plants, books and games, and also kind words. A kind word multiplies friends. A faithful friend is a sturdy shelter – a time to thank God today for those gifts from God through faithful friends. Jesuits, faculty, and students – colleagues. Thank you Lord for the way you reveal yourself through friends.

Faithful indeed you are, friends, in how you show that faithfulness through gathering to visit and pray with me.

—Meditation—
John Cardinal Newman

God has created me to do Him some definite service. He has committed some work to me which He has not committed to another. I have my mission. I may never know it in this life, but I shall be told it in the next. I am a link in a chain, a bond of connection between persons. He has not created me for naught. I shall do good. If I am in sickness, my sickness may serve Him; in perplexity, my perplexity may serve Him; if I am in sorrow, my sorrow may serve Him. He does nothing in vain. He may throw me among strangers. He may make me feel desolate, make my spirit sick, hide my future from me, still He knows what He is about.

—Jeremiah 17:7-8—

Blessed are those who trust in the Lord,
whose trust is in the Lord.
They shall be like a tree planted by water,
sending out its roots by the stream.

—Breastplate of St. Patrick—

May you be blessed with the strength of heaven,
the light of the sun and the radiance of the moon,
and the splendor of fire,
the speed of lightning, the swiftness of wind,
and the depth of the sea,
the stability of earth and the firmness of rock.

Everything in life has something to teach us, if only we allow ourselves to look at it deeply enough.

—Pain and Sacrifice—
Fulton Sheen

There is a very great difference between pain and sacrifice: Pain is sacrifice without love. Sacrifice is pain with love. When we understand this, then we shall have an answer for those who feel that God should have let us sin without pain.

Suffering cleanses us of sin.

When our lease on life runs out there are two qualities that will be asked. The world will ask: How much did he leave? The angels will ask: How much did he bring with him? At death you will leave everything, but there is one thing you will not leave: your desire to live. You want the only thing the Cross brings you. Life through death.

—I Give Thanks—

I heard a wise Jesuit once say that it is impossible to be happy and ungrateful at the same time. My heart is filled with deep gratitude for the gift of life and the way in which Christ lived so powerfully in every aspect during my year of illness.

I give thanks to my God
for all my memories of you,
happy at all times in all
the prayers I offer for
all of you.

And this is my prayer for you:
May your love grow richer
and richer yet, in the fullness
of its knowledge and the
depth of its perception, so
that you may learn to prize what is of value:
may nothing cloud your progress
may you reap through Jesus Christ
the full harvest.
To God's honor and praise.

—The Sending—

Go forth in peace,
have courage,
hold on to what is good,
return no one evil for evil,
strengthen the faint hearted,
support the weak, help the suffering,
honor all men and women,
rejoice in the power of the Holy Spirit.
May Almighty God bless you
in the name of the
Father, Son, and Holy Spirit.